Parenting and The Power of Respect!

By P. Lawrence Wright

Laser Print
Published by Laser Print, Inc.
3483 South West Temple
Salt Lake City, Utah 84115

ISBN: 0-9669717-0-1

Printed by Laser Print, Inc. in the United States of America

Laser Print Paperbacks edition/April 1999

Books are available at quantity discounts for established groups or
organizations promoting parenting counseling, classes or seminars.
For more information please write to The Power of Respect, Laser
Print, Inc., 3483 South West Temple, Salt Lake City, Utah, 84115

First Edition April 1999

To my wonderful
children, Michael,
Sean, Pamela, Elizabeth
and Katie.

It was for you that
I wanted to be a better
parent and because
of you that this book
was possible.

Contents

The importance of respect in our lives and how this instinctive need can be used as a parenting tool for motivating, training and solving discipline problems.

Suggestions for finding ways to show respect to our children. A look at a parent's possible imperfection and exploring possibilities in parenting that use respect as a tool for better communication.

An introduction to the three step system that will allow you to solve discipline problems in a calm and loving way, teaching your children how to choose proper behavior.

Chapter Four:

Examples of problem solving using the three-step system outlined in the previous chapter.

Chapter Five:

Concluding comments by the author reaffirming the importance of non-confrontational parenting and the positive effects of the Power of Respect.

Chapter Six:

A workbook encouraging empathy with your child's problem and for creating consequences customized to fit the personalities of you and your children.

*"The hospital should have given me
a training manual."*

INTRODUCTION

This book is the 'Training Manual' that I wish had been included with the doctor bills, birth certificate and complimentary baby lotion given to my wife when we left the hospital with our first child. Every telephone, toaster and VCR comes with one, but I couldn't find a practical and effective book that applied to the problems I was having with my children. The older they got the bigger the problems became. My children were distancing themselves from me and I was losing control. I was worried for me, I was worried for them and we were all unhappy. I was convinced that there had to be a better way.

What developed was a simple system that not only helped me calmly resolve their behavior problems but also created a closeness that we had never experienced before. This book applies to every brand, make and model of child in need of 'adjustment'.

It doesn't require that you be a perfect parent because allowances are made for imperfection and inconsistency. You won't need to spend weeks reading and studying abstract theories or wondering how to apply them. This book can be read in an evening, the principles applied immediately and dramatic results realized in only days using a 'power' available to every parent. You *can* motivate and teach your children and still have harmony in your home.

Good parenting isn't difficult. Having co-operative children isn't an impossible dream. There exists a system and a power that will make all the hopes and expectations you have ever had for your family and your children, a reality. The power is the Power of Respect. The system is an organized application of respect in dealing with them. Only a parent's emotional problems and lack of self-control will limit the effect of this system and these will be addressed as well.

The purpose of this book is not to convince children to change, but to teach you a new way to deal with them. If you're willing to change to a more effective method, they'll react to that change as a matter of course.

There are five important areas of concern to consider when dealing with your children:

1. Using methods of dealing with them that are based upon mutual respect, with the parent in charge.

2. Communicating to them that you love, support and value them as unique individuals, in both physical and verbal ways.

3. Applying a system of choices and consequences (replacing the system of reward and punishment) that are both logical and natural.

4. A reasonable amount of emotional control communicating that consequences are based upon reason, fairness and justice.

5. Accepting behavior associated with the normal developmental stages of their emotional and physical growth.

All five of these areas will be dealt with in this book. Keep in mind that your success as a parent is going to depend upon your willingness to change parenting methods that you've probably never questioned before, methods that have been used for generations. The results will make it worth the effort.

"It's more important to them than candy."

CHAPTER ONE

Whenever I have the opportunity I enjoy visiting the home of an acquaintance of mine. She has a young daughter that reminds me, now that my own children are older, of how delightful a youngster can be and in the limited time we've spent together, her daughter and I have become great friends.

One evening after a party at her home in California, my friend's husband and I were standing together watching the children play. My little friend came running up to us wanting me to pick her up. She gave me a hug and quickly went to play again. After this happened several times, her father, a strict disciplinarian, turned to me and asked, "What do you do, give her candy?"

"Something like that," I said. But in reality what I gave her was far more desirable than candy. I gave her my attention and my time. When I visited, I noticed her. I began listening to whatever she wanted to tell me before she even knew how to talk. She would babble incoherently and I would nod with interest whenever I felt it appropriate.

The 'candy' I gave her was my respect.

Although I normally tried not to interfere in their parenting problems, there were times that I would quietly cross the line. Getting her daughter ready for bed was usually a trying and frustrating experience. My Friend would ask her daughter to get ready for bed repeatedly but would be ignored. Even gentle threats got no response. Eventually I'd whisper to her youngster "go get ready" and she'd be off like a shot and back in a flash, in her pajamas with her teeth brushed, standing in front of me with a proud smile on her face. She knew I would express pride in her and she was willing to do anything to earn that respect.

To adult and child alike, respect is a basic need, as important as love and nourishment. It motivates our actions and defines who we are and how we relate to the world around us. Because your children will instinctively want and need your respect more than anyone else's it can become the 'candy' that will motivate them to conform to the standards and ideals that you feel are important. Giving them your respect can be, as with my little friend, a powerful way to direct their development, giving you the ability to influence their behavior when all other forms of motivation fail.

The methods outlined in this book are based upon this concept. Express your love for your children constantly, with no reservations or conditions and motivate them by setting realistic standards of behavior that they must meet to earn your respect. Your willingness to grant them this respect, as it's earned, will place at your disposal the motivational tool I call The Power of Respect.

Love and Respect

In order to effectively apply the Power of Respect to alter behavior, the difference between the closely related concepts of love and respect should be clearly understood. Each can be given or withdrawn to influence behavior but will affect the emotional development of your child in different ways.

Love is a strong feeling or emotion causing devoted affection or attachment. Not always rational or understandable, *it does not need to be earned.* This unconditional love, requiring no action, behavior or qualification, should be communicated often to your child. It will give them emotional security and a strong sense of identity, the foundation of self-esteem and self-respect, allowing them to accept life's challenges and problems without fear. In success or failure they must be confident of your love for them.

Respect, however, is a confirmation of a *measurable value* that can be earned or lost by choices and actions without the loss of emotional security. Your love will confirm their existence. Your respect will confirm their value and because they need and want respect so much they will willingly change behavior that does not earn or justify it. If love is the foundation of self-esteem, respect will provide the bricks and mortar.

The Importance of Respect

Reflect on your vocation, whether in the work force or in the home. Ask yourself why you are contented or discontented and the answer will probably be related to the amount of respect you feel you receive for what you do.

We prefer to be treated kindly and certainly enjoy an occasional pat on the back for a job done well. Even simple forms of respect can be as important to us as salary increases or our enjoyment of the work. Without respect for efforts we will inevitably be unhappy in our situations. We have an instinctive desire to be thought of as worth while and valuable.

Successful and happy marriages are products of the application of this concept. Everyday problems can be inflated all out of proportion when we fail to recognize the real issues. Confrontations are not always what they seem to be about. For example, consider the contest that focuses around the commode. Is the position of the toilet seat really so important, or is something else wrong, something harder to identify? It wouldn't really be difficult for husbands to put the seat down and if wives wanted to be considerate wouldn't they want to leave the seat up.

When disagreements of this nature arise someone is crying out for a little consideration and some respect for their concerns. Unfortunately, depending upon how desperately we need verification of our value, we'll sometimes fight to a divorce for what little respect the toilet seat represents.

Respect is also an important consideration in our choice of friends. We look for people who are willing to listen, who will be sympathetic when we're in physical or emotional pain, who'll lend us

*"Maybe the argument is about
something else."*

a hand when no one else has the time, forgive our faults and take our side when assaulted by others. These characteristics imply that there's something special about us, some value we have that might not be obvious to others, and we seek friends who can communicate these feelings of respect. If we have friends it's probably because we treat them the same way. If we could learn to treat our children like we treat our friends, we would have much better relationships with our children.

This idea of respect, even in non-personal relationships, affects us daily and has much to do with the feeling we label happiness. The lower our self-esteem, the greater our need for the esteem of others. What we think will bring us happiness is all too often based upon what others think of us. We sometimes spend more than we earn trying to present an image to others that we think will earn their respect. Strong self-esteem can free us from this expensive quest for a happiness that often eludes us, but as adults it's difficult to create a healthy self-image, an image that should have been developed in our early formative years.

One of the goals we should have as parents is to help our children escape this frustrating dilemma. If we can learn to give our children the respect they earn, they will be happier because happiness is in reality, based upon a strong sense of self-esteem. But because they want our respect so much, we can apply it to more immediate problems. We can use this principle to influence their behavior, and everyone wins!

Motivating with Respect

Your children's need for respect is even greater than your own. Children do not have the maturity or experience to realize that what others think about them is usually unimportant or even self-serving. Their self-esteem depends upon your approval and they crave it more than candy.

Their single most important source of respect must come from you. Although they may turn to other sources if they can't find approval at home, they can be more strongly influenced and motivated by you than by anyone else. Giving your children this respect is a powerful tool that *will* influence their behavior.

It isn't difficult or time consuming to satisfy this craving. It requires an awareness of their needs, an understanding of how to fill those needs, and a sense of self-discipline and self-confidence on your part. Your concern for their emotional well being, complimented by your desire to simplify your life will influence their physical behavior. The first step in this process is to simply become aware that they have feelings too.

Becoming aware that your children are human beings will make it easier to accomplish the goals you've set in fulfilling your responsibilities as a parent. Besides encouraging willing cooperation from your children, you will have the tools necessary to teach them all they will need to know about choices and responsibility, while helping them develop the self-confidence and self-esteem necessary to make their lives more enjoyable and 'successful'. When they eventually leave home it will give them the uninhibited opportunity to pursue happiness in appropriate ways.

Many of us worry about our child's success out-side the home, feeling that the experiences and perceptions of outsiders will become the basis for our child's development of self-esteem. This is only partially true. Although we all have a desire to be accepted by others, treatment from within the family will either validate or negate the feelings of self-worth otherwise earned through outside accomplishments. Very often a child will strive for excellence for the acceptance they have a right to hope will come from their parents. If the parents fail to grant this acceptance the child will gain little.

"We practiced in the dark. We practiced in the rain. It wasn't fun."

When my children were younger I understood the importance of helping them develop their self-esteem but, unfortunately, the early methods I chose actually destroyed the very confidence I was hoping to build. My oldest son, Michael, suffered the most.

Being an athlete myself, I felt that sports would provide an opportunity to teach Mike skills that, appreciated by others, would help him feel good about himself, and so I insisted that he participate in Little League. Large for his age, Mike hadn't fully developed his coordination and sometimes had difficulty learning the necessary skills, never really enjoying the experience. Sensing that it was important to me, he went at it with all the enthusiasm that a child needing the love and respect of his father could hope to muster. Instead of praising his efforts I decided that if he didn't excel, he wouldn't gain the confidence that I felt he needed and so I started putting pressure on him. I knew that if I acted disappointed or even angry, he would try even harder to earn my love.

After every practice or game I would chide him for his mistakes and criticize every move he'd made. I dragged him outside for special practices to work on his skills. We practiced in the rain, in the cold and in the dark. It wasn't fun.

Someday I hope to have the patience that he displayed during those 'Little League' years. After all the aggravation and frustration, after straining our relationship to the breaking point, he had less self-esteem than when we started. I finally had to admit that the entire program on my part was a dismal failure. I'd forgotten the purpose of the whole thing...to develop his self-esteem. Instead we spent three years destroying it.

In later years Michael became involved in dramatics, a pursuit that he chose. He soon was full of the confidence that I had wanted for him, developing it by participating in the activities that he enjoyed and strengthened with my unconditional love and communication that his father was proud of him. I had finally learned that my approval was more important than his level of skill and that too much pressure and too much criticism offset any gains that his successes might have otherwise developed.

The methods I had been using with my son were about as useful as trying to hang a picture with a wreaking ball. I was lucky. Before too much damage was done, I made changes and Michael and our relationship survived.

The Carrot on a stick

Once there was a man who owned a stubborn mule. In order to get the mule to pull his cart, the man tied a stick to it's harness and with a string, dangled a carrot just out of the reach of the mule's waiting lips. All day long the mule walked toward that carrot, not wise enough to realize that the carrot would always be just beyond it's grasp.

Our children are smarter than that mule.

Whether you realize it or not, your children are trying hard to earn your approval. Accepting their efforts without giving them their reward is just like dangling a carrot in front of that mule. How effective the carrot will be as motivation will depend upon too things: how much your children want it and whether or not they ever get it. Some parents discover how effectively they can motivate their children by offering approval (respect), and then withholding that approval to further motivate them. Any 'carrot on a stick' strategy used to motivate children will eventually fail.

After years of working very hard to earn their reward, they will eventually learn that they're never going to get it. It's then that they stop trying, but not because they lose their desire for your approval. They just give up in frustration.

"Our children are smarter than that mule."

The way I was trying to motivate Mike was just such a system. I was offering to approve of him if he'd learn some particular baseball skill but instead of approving of him I was requiring more effort instead. Not only was he losing his desire to play baseball, he was beginning to learn that no matter how hard he tried, he might never be worthy of my respect. I was losing the control that the 'carrot on a stick' method had provided me and he was becoming withdrawn, depressed, argumentative and unhappy. The way I was using the 'carrot ' was damaging and unsuccessful but it wasn't the only ineffective motional tool in my bag of tricks. I was an expert at an even more destructive method. I could be very intimidating.

Intimidation

There's a debate in parenting circles today about the effectiveness and effects of corporal punishment (spanking) on children. I now personally feel that it's not only damaging but represents only one form of a much larger parenting problem, intimidation.

Intimidation takes many forms, but the idea behind any of them is the communication that we parents are larger and stronger and are willing to use that advantage to force our will on our chil-

"Intimidation can leave scars on your children that can last a lifetime."

dren. It's simply control using the threat of physical or emotional injury as motivation.

We can express that threat in many ways, from violence to direct threats of violence, to more subtle non-verbal threats of violence like the 'look' I created to deal with my youngest daughter Katie.

When Katie was four years old, I had an experience with her that although I found it to be cute at the time, made me realize the effect that even subtle intimidation was having on her.

At dinner one night I must have been unhappy with something she was doing. As I looked at her she began to tremble and said, "Don't look at me like that." I asked her what she meant and her response was to look at me with the same expression that I had used. I couldn't help but laugh. There was a little 'me' looking across the table with my scowl of disapproval on her face.

I never realized that my look was just as intimidating and frightening to her as an angry verbal or physical threat would have been. Of course I'd developed the 'look' to achieve that very result, but I didn't like it looking back at me. I wanted to be close to my children. Fear wasn't an acceptable substitute.

If intimidation is a major part of the relationship you have with your children and they're young, you're probably finding that it's pretty effective. If it didn't get results it wouldn't be as popular as it is. But before it's too late you might want to ask yourself how you plan to control them when they're too big to threaten.

If it hasn't happened to you already, the day is going to come that your child will take the 'stick' out of your hand and inform you that you have just lost your power to control them. The system of intimidation has a side effect. It becomes obsolete!

Influence or Control

As I've been using the terms control and influence to describe how we motivate our children, you might have noticed that I don't use them interchangeably, even though the definitions are similar. In an attempt to communicate the mental attitude required to apply the Power of Respect, I've redefined these words and reassigned them a positive and negative value.

The word control has always had an ominous connotation for me. Prisoners are controlled. Slaves are controlled. Control is used when the feelings of the object of that control are unimportant or of little significance.

18

Influence, however, suggests that the object to whom it's directed has rights, feelings and some power to choose, and it's this definition that communicates that we think of our children as important and worthwhile individuals, capable not only of making proper choices but of accepting responsibility for those choices.

While under your care, the choices that they'll be making will be limited of course, but through this process they'll be learning to deal with the choices and responsibilities that will become a larger part of their lives as they mature. If for your own convenience you attempt to simply control their behavior, they'll have little opportunity to develop the problem solving skills that they'll need as adults. And eventually they'll reject your attempts to control them.

There's a natural instinct in the human spirit that inevitably leads us all to the conclusion that control and responsibility are inseparable. He who wields control should also shoulder the responsibility. It's wonderful to be able to make all the choices and allow someone else to suffer the consequences. Of course it's frustrating to be the one who must suffer the burdens of those choices without the power to make the changes necessary to avoid the consequences. It's easy to accept the results of the choices we make but most of us will rebel if we're constantly forced to suffer consequences that occur due to the choices of others. Our children will react in the same way.

Influence, however, allows choices and the consequences of those choices to be determined by the person they most affect. If you want to have any influence on your child in their teen and adult lives, start thinking in terms of how you can *influence* their choices and avoid the pitfalls created by control.

In Conclusion

A war is being fought for the minds and bodies of our children. Many of us are losing the battle and don't even know how to fight back. Use the Power of Respect! The forces with designs on them are using it to lure them into their control, but they can only succeed if we fail. These people are satisfied with our castoffs, our rejects and our failures. They want the children that we're throwing away. Our children want our approval and respect but they'll settle for whatever they can get from whatever the source, good or bad.

Give your children the respect they so desperately want. Once they realize that you're willing to give it to them they'll be willing to work for it, behave for it, in fact they'll be willing to do almost anything for it.

When an adult shows a lack of respect for a child it's considered their right as a parent. When the child demands respect or develops 'behavior' problems, parents conclude that they have an unmanageable child on their hands.

If your children are normal they'll come to want the same respect that you do. If you're unwilling or unable to give it to them, sooner or later they will rebel. Learn to motivate your children with the Power of Respect rather than the power of intimidation and soon you'll have the happy home that you might have come to feel was only possible in your dreams.

If you find it difficult to treat your children with respect, it could be that you have problems that must be resolved. The following chapter addresses some of the parenting skills that will most effectively express respect to your child. If you tend to be uncomfortable with critical self-evaluation you might not be comfortable with what you discover. Your child might not be the only one with skills to learn.

"Parents need to grow up too."

CHAPTER TWO:
Parents need to grow up too

While working as a counselor for juvenile delinquents at a special school in Provo, Utah, I was often frustrated to see that while the methods we used were often successful, the students usually reverted back to old behavior problems when they returned home. If their parents treated them in the same old way, and their friends treated them in the same old way, they reacted the same way that they always had.

While they were with us, I came to love and care about them. However the frustration of such a low permanent success rate, about 20%, finally motivated me to leave the profession. What I learned was that the children weren't "bad" children or uncontrollable. It was the system that they lived in and were developing in that was ineffective.

There are innocent mistakes that parents can make without realizing the effect they have on their children. The youth I worked with generally had parents that were good people that loved their families but few of the parents could see the effect their actions had on the behavior of their children. The parents wanted their children to change without having to make changes themselves. Because a discipline problem is a family problem, the counselors, psychologists and sociologists at the school counseled both the parents and their children. We were able to convince most of the youth that our system was a better system, but we often failed when we addressed the behavior of the parents. If the parents refuse to change there could be little permanent success.

You must be willing to change. Improvement in parent/child relationships begins when parents find better way to interact with their children. *It needs to start with you!*

Your children are going to respond to the methods that you use to deal with them. Poor methods will produce poor results. Temper problems, unrealistically high expectations, constant criticism, over reacting or reacting without thinking, and confused messages of what you actually expect of them are mistakes that are easy to make. Even if you make these mistakes for all the right reasons, they will produce negative results with your children. An effort to learn and apply better techniques will bring about a corresponding change in your children that will surprise you. If you're having problems with your child, the first assumption you should learn to make is that it might be your fault.

This chapter deals with problems common to most parents. Evaluate yourself honestly and make an effort to change if necessary. The job of changing the behavior of your children begins with you. You might never be a perfect parent but that's okay. If you're willing to take the first step, your children will meet you half way.

Because this book is intended to teach you how to harness the Power of Respect, the following suggestions are related to parent problems that most affect the communication of that principle. I'm sure that as you try the system and see the effect that it has on your children, you'll become anxious to discover more on your own. Just try to see problems from your child's point of view and treat them the way you would like to be treated.

Temper

Have you ever gotten angry with your children when they lose their temper? If losing your temper when they've lost theirs seems hypocritical to you, you probably have the common sense it takes to be a good parent.

The 'do as I say, not as I do' method of raising children has it's drawbacks. You might be able to get away with it when your children are young, but teenagers have an annoying habit of noticing things like that. They won't think it's fair and will wonder if you know what you're talking about. They'll be right to wonder.

In any other area of their lives, anger will be considered disrespectful. In dealing with your child's discipline problems it is counter productive as well. Although it might seem to be the easiest way to control them, it teaches a principle that will not serve them as adults, that somehow age determines when anger is acceptable. It's also true that as they grow older, it's effectiveness as a control measure diminishes and actually adds to the normally difficult problems they'll be facing as teens. Worst of all, constant intimidation is destructive to their self-esteem, something they'll need plenty of as they grow older. If you want to avoid aggravating the problems that you might have with your teenagers, try to control your temper when dealing with them.

Listening

From the age that your children start to babble incoherently, take the time to listen. They need your respect even at that early age. Remember that they are people too, small and messy perhaps, but important people none-the-less. As they become older and they want to tell a joke, stop and listen. If they want to share their accomplishments or tell you about some new and exciting information that they've just learned, even if you already know about it, listen. If they want to share their problems with you, count your blessings and listen. You don't have to offer solutions. Many times they don't even want your solutions. They just want you to be there and care.

If you don't take the opportunity to listen, the day will come that they'll stop trying to talk to you. Communication problems don't begin because someone doesn't want to talk. More than likely it's because no one is listening. Don't let that happen. Take the time to listen.

Understand Their feelings

When my son Sean was in the first grade he began to have problems at school. He normally loved school but all of a sudden he was coming up with any excuse he could think of to stay home. I asked him if there was a problem but he just wouldn't talk about it.

Being aware that his behavior was out of the ordinary, I tried to listen to more than what he was saying. I asked him questions attempting to find out what the real problem was and tried to sympathize with any problem I could even imagine might be causing the trouble. I would suggest that the kids in the schoolyard play pretty rough sometimes. He would tell me that wasn't the problem and I would guess again.

After I had convinced him that I could sympathize with just about any problem he had, he finally opened up. It seems that because he finished his work so quickly, the teacher was making him put his head on the desk and wait for the other kids to catch up. He thought he was being punished and was embarrassed to tell me about it. Understanding that the problem was more than he was willing to talk about allowed us to solve it.

Sometimes, just like Sean, your child will cry out for help but because of guilt, embarrassment or just an inability to find the right words, won't be able to communicate effectively. That's when you need to do the hardest type of listening. The kind that lets you hear what they're feeling and not necessarily what they're saying.

Perfection

We all feel that our own children should be the smartest and most talented in the entire world and that there should be no excuse for them to be less than perfect in all things. But reality dictates that they all can't be the best.

Why is it that we sometimes find it difficult to be content with the best that our children can do? How many SoapBox Derby cars, children's cake baking contests and even some school science projects look like they were really constructed by children? Sometimes we even actually push our children aside and do things for them, rather than accept the fact that children need time to perfect their talents. If they aren't allowed to do the work they won't learn and they won't get the joy and satisfaction from a job well done. Try to allow your children to do the best they can, even with mistakes, and praise the effort.

*"How many Soap Box Derby cars look like
they were built by children?"*

There are great lessons to be learned from mistakes they discover on their own. The older they get the more serious and painful the lessons learned, so let them learn at an early age. And don't be disappointed when your pride and joy proves to be as human as the rest of us. It's not a reflection on you as a parent. It's normal.

Goals

Whenever you help your children set goals, set high goals but let perfection be a little bit higher. Imagine their joy when they exceed your expectations and even better, imagine yours!

Criticism

Don't criticize everything that your children do. Accept some things as they are, praise them for what they did accomplish and let it go. They'll get better with practice and all the extra pressure you put on them will only serve to dampen their desire to try again.

Above all be careful that the criticism is justified. When I was in the ninth grade I was in my room studying one night. My mother burst into the room and began to scold me for not studying. She yelled at me for about a half an hour and wouldn't

"She interrupted my studying to scold me for not studying."

listen to anything I had to say in my defense. I didn't do any homework again until my second year in college! I knew that she was wrong and decided that if I was going to be yelled at for something, it might as well be justified. She could have handled it better. Not only didn't she get the result that she was after; she made the situation much worse.

Be careful with your criticism and try to praise your children more than you censure them. It'll be more effective and you'll be more fun to be around.

Think ahead

It isn't always necessary to point out every flaw, correct every mistake or discipline every problem. Evaluate the situation first. Hasty actions can often make things worse. A good example of this occurred while Christmas shopping with my niece and nephew.

Peter wasn't feeling well and was taking it out on his sister. I tried to be patient, but in fairness to Jamie, the time came for me to get involved. The problem wasn't going to go away. I could see that in his mood he wasn't going to stop just because I asked him to. Getting angry with him would have obviously made things worse, so I decided to be understanding.

I told him that I could see that he didn't feel well, (true) and that he looked really tired, (also true) so I offered to get him something to drink at the snack area. I suggested that Jamie continue shopping and meet us there when she was ready. It didn't take long for Peter to calm down on his own. It's hard to be angry with someone trying to sympathize with you. By the time Jamie returned he was feeling fine and we all enjoyed the rest of our shopping.

You can do the same thing with your children. If they're tired, bored or just in a bad mood for no good reason, it might be best to overlook the problem and distract them in some clever way. They might forget what they're doing and solve the problem for you.

You could consider that it might be illness that causes them to 'act up' and there's always the possibility that it might be you that's in the bad mood and just being too sensitive. I've saved myself many a headache by looking for solutions that don't require confrontation. Try to evaluate the situation before you act, be realistic and look before you leap.

Praise

Sometimes we concentrate so much on damage control (bad behavior) that we overlook the opportunity to do preventative maintenance (praising good behavior). Just like oiling machinery to keep it running properly, we need to praise our children before things go wrong. Never pass up an opportunity to reward behavior that pleases you. You can praise part of an accomplishment even if you aren't pleased with the whole.

My daughter Elizabeth has always been an excellent student. So much so that I began to take it for granted. One report period she came home with a report card that had all A's but one (gasp) B. When I saw that, you must know what I did. I complained. How did she dare get a B? Wasn't she trying anymore? Didn't she care? I really hurt her. All this time she had been working as hard as she could and I didn't bother to say anything until she slipped. There's nothing wrong with a B, but more important was the fact that she should have been praised for the A's, even if the other grade was an F.

If you learn to let praise dominate your relationship with your children, you're going to discover that they'll be more receptive to criticism when it becomes necessary. Don't let them think

"She should have been praised for the A's."

that you see only the bad. You might end up convincing them that they're incapable of anything else. Find ways to let them know how proud you are of them whenever it's deserved. Let them know that you noticed. Lack of punishment is not a reward. Acknowledge good behavior.

Gratitude

Children deserve to be thanked, even for what they're expected to do. This is a painless way to show respect.

Apologize

This is a painful way to show respect but children deserve to hear that you too can make a mistake especially in dealing with them. None of us will be a perfect parent and our children don't expect us to be. They'll quickly forgive and forget if we let them know that we hold ourselves to the same standards that we expect of them. Wrong is wrong no matter who is wrong.

Let them be right sometimes

Try not to confuse a 'right' way with the 'best' way. Sometimes the way they want to do something will work just fine.

Working in Civic Theater has been a hobby of mine for a number of years now, and an experience a dear friend of mine had there, demonstrates the problem that can be caused by too much direction.

My friend was helping build a set for the summer stock performance of South Pacific. She was building the shower stall for the "wash that man right out of my hair" scene and was doing just fine. She might have been using a little more material than was necessary and her way was going to take a little more time to construct than another way might have but there was going to be nothing wrong with the final result.

About this time the technical director passed through and decided that he wanted her to do it his way. Without thinking, he told her that she was doing it wrong and explained to her how he wanted it done. My friend was offended. She decided that if he didn't trust her and wanted to get that involved, he could tell her exactly where each nail and each drop of glue should be placed. Not surprisingly the work ground to a halt.

Our children will often react the same way. By trying to make them do something the 'best' way, we might be communicating the message that we think their way is wrong. In order to gain confidence in themselves, they need to be allowed to be right sometimes. Let them.

Listen for content / ignore the tone

I was in a bad mood one night and needed to blow off some steam. My daughter Pamela became my target. She was enjoying a quiet evening, staying out of trouble and minding her own business when I attacked her with all the fervor that an adult adolescent (me) could muster.

I accused her of one thing and then another. She stood there listening until I finished and then went back to her room. I went about my business.

After about 15 minutes she came back out, now full of the anger I had transferred to her, and began to give it back. She said, "Dad, you're wrong!" My first reaction was to take offense, not only at the tone of her voice but from the idea that I might be wrong! Children aren't supposed to talk to their parents like that. Fortunately, before I started to yell back I began to listen. She was defending herself and she was right.

I had accused her of things that I thought were true but as she continued to loudly refute what I had said, I began to realize that I had been unfair.

But what about the tone of her voice? Could I just ignore that?

Sure. Why not? There was a principle involved far more important than that. She felt she was right and was willing to stand up for herself. After she had her say, she went back to her room and I did some more thinking. I finally followed her and apologized. I told her that I was proud of her for having the courage to defend herself, gave her a hug and then we had a chance to discuss better ways that each of us could have handled the situation. We both learned something and had grown closer in the process.

Try not to fall into the trap of reacting to the tone of their voice. Listen to what they're trying to communicate and deal with the tone later.

Team work

It's important that a parent in conflict with a child be allowed to resolve the problem without interference from another parent. They must be permitted to come to a resolution and have a chance to love the child better before the other parent offers comfort. Afterwards, a little extra love could never hurt.

IN CONCLUSION

It's okay that parents might need to grow up. If you can learn to accept that and communicate the possibility that you too can have problems, your children will feel more comfortable coping with their own. Besides, you can't fool them forever. Cushion the surprise that will surely come the day they realize how human you are, and avoid having to defend the perfection that even they will be able to see doesn't really exist.

"It's as easy as One-Two-Three."

CHAPTER THREE:
It's as Easy As One-Two-Three"

In order to function in an orderly manner society establishes rules and a system to enforce those rules. What is expected of each individual is made clear and a consequence provided for those who choose noncompliance. This can be an effective system if administered properly and necessary if you expect your home to run in an orderly way.

The problem in dealing with children is that the rules change and new situations arise. As they grow older more is expected. Communicating and updating these changes becomes a parent's greatest challenge but is also the key to any system that will establish order in your home.

The one-two-three step method used in this book is the most effective way to resolve these problems. Your children will feel more comfortable, and will cooperate more readily in a changing environment when they know what's expected of them and exactly what will happen if they choose not to conform.

The younger they are, the more they'll want to please you, but often they're confused by the complexity of the expectations or your inconsistent reactions. This system will help you communicate the ever-changing rules in a peaceful, loving and understandable manner.

Once you understand how to use the system and begin to apply it regularly, your children will quickly learn to recognize it and react to it in a positive way. It won't always be fun for them but they'll come to accept it as fair, and they'll be able to live with that. More importantly, however, it will help you communicate what you expect of them and the consequences should they fail to comply. The choice will be theirs and it won't take long before they'll willingly choose to comply.

The system

The system you'll be using when dealing with discipline problems consists of three steps. They will be the method of communicating your requests to your children. Your ability to properly use all three steps in order will determine how effective the system will be in your family. They're intended to convince your children that you mean what you say, but in an orderly, peaceful, fair and impartial manner. You are no longer going to be a combatant, fighting for peace and order, but rather a referee in their struggle with life.

Once the system is initiated, it must be carried to its conclusion. If the problem is important enough to warrant your attention, you must endure to the end. Once you've communicated your determination to change to this new method, you'll begin to be the recipient of cooperation that you've seldom noticed before. Because the system is based on kindness and respect, this cooperation will happen before you find it necessary to raise your voice and corporal punishment will never be necessary.

The system is initiated with you asking nicely, followed by defining their choices and concluded, as necessary, with an appropriate consequence. All three steps are important. Once you start, be prepared to finish, always starting with step one.

STEP ONE

The Signal: Ask nicely.

This is the most important step! It sounds simple enough but it is too often forgotten when we deal with our children. You shouldn't expect them to cooperate willingly if you seldom give them the chance. Ask nicely, using a friendly tone of voice and maybe they'll do it.

Steps Two and Three will give you all the influence you want but with more positive effects than intimidation will create. Step One is intended to signal that the system has been put into effect and cannot be stopped except by your child's cooperation. If you want to establish harmony in your home, *you* must be harmonious. Step One must be kind and loving. Ask nicely!

STEP TWO

The Options

If after all of your efforts to be nice, your children have refused, complained or failed to do what you've asked of them, it's time to teach them that they're making the wrong choice. Before drastic measures are taken, however, it's important that all of the options are explained to them and their choices defined.

Step Two defines their options. Maintaining your pleasant tone, you now need to explain to them that they can still choose to do what you have asked, but if they refuse, complain or fail to do it, a consequence will follow. The consequence you choose should be described to them at this time. It must be related to the problem and neither too lenient or too severe. The next chapter will have detailed examples for specific situations but the following will give you the basic idea.

Example One: If they should abuse the rules for riding their bicycle, the consequence could be that their riding privileges would be revoked for a period of time.

Example Two: If they fail to complete a job, extra jobs would be assigned.

It wouldn't make sense to revoke their bicycle privileges for not doing the dishes. It will be easier for them to accept consequences that are logical and fit the situation. In Step Two you'll need to clearly explain what's expected, determine fair consequences and be ready to go to Step Three if Steps One and Two have failed.

STEP THREE

The Consequences

If after Step Two your child still refuses to co-operate, you must enforce the consequence. It is critical at this point that you follow through. Your children must be convinced that the choices they make will lead to the conclusion you promised, good or bad. If they think that there is even a small chance that they will avoid something they don't like by resisting you, they will continue to resist. This is exactly the behavior you want to change, so be strong, and enforce the consequence.

Be loving, be sympathetic, but finish what you start. You gave them every opportunity by explaining the options and outlining the choices. Now it's time to teach them that it will always be best to choose properly. Be strong. Always follow through!

In Conclusion

Applying these steps every time you face a confrontation with your children will get you all the cooperation you have ever wanted. It will get easier as time goes by, so stick with it. Soon you'll be a positive and pleasant influence in their lives, free of the frustration you always felt was a normal part of parenting. Keep these three steps in mind.

Step One: *The signal.* Ask nicely. This step lets your children know that the system is in effect.

Step Two: *The options.* This step defines their choices and describes the consequences.

Step Three: *The consequence.* This step is intended to convince them that it would always be best to avoid Step Three.

NOTE: I suggest that from time to time you record your experiences with your children on a tape recorder. When you are alone, listen to it as if your voice belonged to a stranger and evaluate the tone of voice *you* used in the interaction. There are times that you might sound angry when you didn't intend to. Practice sounding nice, kind and calm when dealing with your children's problems. This system requires that you be 'nice' and it starts with the tone of *your* voice.

"Apply the system to everyday problems."

CHAPTER FOUR:
Solving Some Problems

In order for you to see how well the system works you'll want to actually apply it to everyday problems. This chapter includes some common problems and possible solutions that use the One-Two-Three Step System as well as other techniques. All apply the principle of respect.

I have only gone to Step Three two times with any of my children but I've had to explain the options and potential consequences more than that. Determining logical consequences turned out to be the most challenging part of the system but became easier with experience.

These examples are intended to show you how the system works so that you can begin to create solutions on your own. It would be impossible to anticipate all the problems that might arise with your children so only a sample few are included, but the principle will be the same no matter what the problem. Have fun with these and be ready to create additional solutions of your own. Keep the following four principles in mind:

1. The problems your children are having are normal. They aren't trying to anger or frustrate you. Please note that the introduction to each of these examples attempts to understand the reasons that the problem exists. Respect begins before you start to deal with the situation. Your calm and understanding attitude will communicate concern for the behavior of the child and will not be interpreted as an attack on their value as an individual. It will help you influence their behavior without destroying their self-esteem or your relationship with them.

2. The second part of the example will be the application of the system outlined in Chapter Three. Consequences are proposed but are not the only possibilities. You might have better ideas of your own based upon your knowledge of your child. Their age and abilities should be considered, remembering above all, that fairness *and* justice must pre-

vail. The goal is to correct a problem. Your attitude and actions must reflect that principle. This must not become an outlet for your anger or frustration.

3. At first you might have difficulty determining logical and effective consequences. These examples are intended to help you get started, but you should begin to develop the ability to create others on your own as soon as possible. With practice it will become second nature.

4. Remember to use all three steps as necessary and apply these solutions with love and respect. Soon it will be difficult for you to remember when dealing with your children was a challenge.

 **GOING TO BED:
" The party's over"**

There will come a time in your child's young life when he or she will decide to determine their own bedtime. They'll discover that staying up late could be great fun, and they weren't tired anyway, thank you very much.

In determining your child's bedtime remember that all children have different sleep requirements and yours might need more or less sleep than others. If they go to bed later than you think

"Turn out the lights, the party's over."

appropriate but wake up each morning without any problem, you may need to make an adjustment.

Once you've considered their physical needs it's all right to consider your needs. As an adult and parent you're entitled to quiet and private time in the evening without interruptions from your children. If you want this free time you'll want to teach them to respect your needs and correct the bedtime hassle once-and-for-all. Very quietly and always under complete control, try it like this:

Step One: Ask nicely

Ask them politely to go to bed.

Step Two: The choices

If they refuse, ask them again adding that if they don't they'll have to stay up until you decide they can go to bed. Warn them that they won't be able to play or watch television, but if they choose to stay up they can stay with you. They'll probably think that they've gotten what they wanted, but soon they'll know better.

Step Three: The consequence

If they've chosen to stay up, take them to a quiet place and start reading a book, sewing, writing working at the computer, washing dishes or any activity that they'll consider dull and uninteresting. Then begin to work.

Don't discuss things with them, cuddle with them or do anything that might make this a fun experience. And especially don't allow them to go to sleep! *Always be nice* but don't do anything that will reward them for their unacceptable behavior.

Soon they'll become weary of the adventure and will probably ask if they can do something more entertaining. Don't let them. You're trying to get them bored enough to want to go to bed.

Finally they'll decide that even bed would be more interesting. Don't let them go to bed yet. They gave up the right to make that decision, at least for tonight, and you're not going to let them go to bed until they want it very, very much. It won't take long before your child will begin to plead with you to let them go to bed. They might even begin to cry. Be strong. This is the moment you've been waiting for.

Now you can ask them if they're sure that this is what they want. When they sob that it is, let them come over to you so that you can hug them and reaffirm your love for them. Then take them to bed. Once they're in bed, you can cuddle, kiss and hug them for a few minutes, and then all that's left is to turn out the lights, the party's over.

Although the problem may reoccur the next night, simply remind them what happened the night before, asking them if they really want you to decide their bedtime for them. If they persist, go to Step Two and repeat it again. Soon they'll know that when you say go to bed now, you mean now. They may not go to bed with a smile on their face but that's okay because there's going to be one on yours.

2 BEDTIME REQUESTS: "Will it never end?"

Even after your children are in bed they don't always understand why they're there. They want one more drink of water or have one more thing to say. Their demands can go on forever.

The way to resolve this problem is to plan. Try to anticipate every request they might have before they go to bed. Each night they ask for something new, make a note of it and prepare for it the next night. As you tuck them in, go through the list explaining that after they're in bed you won't be responding to any of their requests. You need to convince them that if they need anything, they

"Stranger things have happened."

have to get it before you leave them alone for the night.

Once they're in bed, don't pay any attention to them. If they discover that you'll come running every time they holler, they'll keep on hollering. To them it's a game to play with mom or dad until they get really sleepy. If you don't want to play, then don't. In a couple of nights they'll get tired of a game that only they play and it will end.

Because these cries for attention are just that, give them as much attention as you can just before you put them to bed. Snuggle, cuddle, hug and talk, but let them know that when you leave their bedroom, you won't be back until morning.

This isn't considered a discipline problem so the Three Step system isn't needed. If they get up, however, refer to the bedtime solution and reestablish a routine for going to bed that they understand. Don't get upset. As soon as they understand, the game will end.

3 FEAR OF THE DARK: "Check the Closet."

Try to remember when you were young. Don't you remember when every shadow on the wall was a stranger in your room? The clothes rack was a monster waiting until you were asleep before eating you. The floor was covered with snakes and everything was all right unless the lights went out. Well, now your kids are kids and have the same natural fears that you had. Just play along. Be understanding and realize that an adult's reason doesn't work for kids. So what do you do? You've explained everything as well as you could and they still want the lights left on. Leave them on. They'll grow out of it. They're not wimps. They're normal.

If the problem seems serious or if your children are in their twenties you might take a few extra preventative precautions. Don't let them watch movies that feed their fears. If you think it's cute to see them frightened at a movie, you might as well think it's cute for them to be afraid of the dark at bedtime. If you tell them scary stories, expect them to be scared.

The more reassuring you can be, the sooner they'll get over their fear of the dark. Knowing that you're close and will protect them will help, but before you leave their room check the closet. Maybe there is something in there. Stranger things have happened.

TEMPER TANTRUMS:
"The king meets his match"

Putting an end to your child's temper tantrums can be fun. The solution is a one-time experience that will bring to a close the era of tantrums in your home. It requires a little play-acting on your part and will mean that you set aside your anger and frustration temporarily, but the results are amazing and the experience down right enjoyable.

Although each of my children have had short lived temper tantrums, the most dramatic demonstration occurred with Sean, a neighbor's four-year-old child. He was wonderful, bright, enthusiastic, energetic, and normally enjoyable to be around. Little did I know that he was the king of temper tantrums.

Sean was by far, the youngest of three children. He was treated a little more protectively than the others and as a result, discovered some interesting ways to manipulate the people around him. I suppose it was easier to give in to him than to endure his tirades, but this was about to end. The king of temper tantrums was about to meet his match!

One day we all decided to go play some baseball. Sean was batting when the time came to leave, but I offered to let him hit five more first. I

"The king of temper tantrums was about to meet his match."

counted as he hit, but when we got down to the last one, he stopped, held up all of his fingers (he didn't know how to count yet) and said "This many." I replied that we were in a hurry and needed to go. That's when he started into his routine.

He cried, fell to the ground, screamed and just would not listen. Brian, his older brother, and I finally gave up trying to reason with him and started toward the car. As we turned the corner at the end of the fence, little Sean stopped his tantrum, came running over and once again in view, began all over again.

Back down in the dirt he went, arms and legs flailing. Brian, angry, frustrated and embarrassed, was about to force Sean to go to the car, but I stopped him. This was the first time Sean had tried his tantrum on me and I wanted to convince him that he was wasting his time. In fact I had been waiting for just this opportunity. I told Brian to watch and learn.

As I walked over to where Sean was 'performing', I kept my eyes riveted on his every move. Once I was close enough, I stopped and gave him all of my attention and began to praise him, expressing wonder at his technique. I told him that I had never seen anyone do better, that I had five children of my own and none of them were as good as he was at having a temper tantrum. My whole demeanor expressed wonder at his skill. Then I began to coach him.

He was pounding his arms with his fists balled up, so in a helpful manner I suggested that if he would slap the ground with his palms down, the affect would be much better. At that point he started flinging his arms back and forth in the dirt and began to raise a cloud of dust that could be seen for miles. That really impressed me and I told him so. I even turned to his brother and asked if he was seeing all of this. Brian was in the car laughing.

About then something happened that almost started me laughing. Sean actually started to add my suggestions to his tantrum, looking at me with an expression that seemed to ask, "Who is this guy?" At that point I knew that I had him. Although he was still going through the motions, he had lost a lot of his enthusiasm and had even stopped screaming. I thanked him for showing me what he could do, and started back to the car. As I walked away from him, I asked him to join us, and he did! Thanking him again, I gave him a hug and we have been best buddies ever since.

It was interesting that after we returned to his house something occurred with his mother that started him having another tantrum. As his mother started to deal with it, Brian excitedly interrupted her and said, "Let me do it. I want to show you something that I learned from Larry."

He went through the same routine with Sean that I had, with the same results. I never saw Sean throw another tantrum, at least he never tried it with me, and it was accomplished without anger, frustration or threats. It was simply a creative application of the principle of respect and the result was the end of behavior that I found to be offensive. He was happy, I was happy and the problem was resolved.

As you apply this technique, you will want to follow this basic plan:

1. Become interested in what your child is doing. Give them your attention in a positive way. Don't communicate to them that in reality you feel angry, frustrated or in the slightest way tempted to give them what they want.

2. Praise them for being the very best at having tantrums. Act as if you are in awe of their ability but be helpful and make suggestions that you feel might improve their tantrum skills. Your tone of

*"No matter how big the job seems to them,
teach them that it could be worse."*

voice is the most useful tool at this time. While they are screaming they might not be able to hear or understand your words, but the friendly, helpful, calm tone and attitude will let them know that something is different and it will eventually get their attention.

3. Once you notice that the energy has slackened from their performance or their expression has changed from anger to wonder or confusion, thank them again and suggest an alternate activity. It can be something fun or not. As you turn and walk away, invite them to go with you. When they follow, stop and give them a big hug. I know that they will want to give you one and you'll deserve it.

5 DOING THE JOB: "It could be worse"

Getting your children to help around the house can often be more difficult and time consuming than doing the work yourself. Cleaning up is necessary, however, and someone's going to have to do it. If you've finally decided that it isn't always going to be you, you should be ready to apply the system and start getting all the help you deserve. It might me a little more complicated than in some other discipline problems because your child's re-actions to your requests are going to differ and you'll have to be ready to cover each possibility. I've outlined three examples but the method is the same in each. The first covers the refusal to work, the second shows how to respond when they agree to help but don't, and the third explains how to deal with the child that never seems to finish.

Example A:
"No, but thanks for asking."

Step 1: Ask them politely to do the chore.

Step 2: If they refuse to do it or complain, re-peat your request adding that if they think that what you've asked seems too much or unfair, you will give them an additional job besides. Explain to them that each time they refuse or complain, you plan to add another job.

Step 3: If they still refuse, assign another chore to do after they complete the first. Each time they complain or refuse, give them another job, all of which have to be completed before they can go about their own business. Once they start working let them know how happy you are that they finally made the right choice.

After they finish the original task, expect them to ask if they really have to do the extra jobs. You had better answer yes or you won't have accomplished anything. Follow through properly and one time should be enough.

Example B:
"Sure, but don't hold your breath."

Step 1: Ask nicely.

Step 2: If they agree to do the job, but you later find that it wasn't done, ask them again explaining that you now require that it be finished by some specific time. You determine when that will be, limited only by your kindness and patience. You should also tell them that if it isn't done, they won't be allowed whatever it was that has been distracting them from performing the task at hand. If they argue or complain refer to Example A.

Step 3: Check at the predetermined time and if the work hasn't been finished, apply the consequence. If the work doesn't seem to be progressing, refer to Example C.

Example C:
"Maybe it will go away."

Step 1: All of my children, having been convinced that they can't refuse or complain about doing a job,

"The only 'escape' is to finish."

have come to the conclusion that if they procrastinate long enough, some magic will make the job go away. I've assigned them kitchen duty and found them in the kitchen hours later with no work accomplished. Since they already knew what it was that they were supposed to do and had agreed to do it, I would progress to step two.

Step 2: At this time I explained to them that the work had to be done no matter how long it took. I warned them that if they didn't begin soon they wouldn't be allowed to leave the area for any reason until the job was finished and that it didn't matter to me how long that was.

Step 3: If you have gotten to this point with one of your children and they still haven't accomplished anything when you return, tell them that they cannot leave the room except to go to the bathroom and then only after they ask permission. It helps to have a geographical boundary such as the kitchen proper because it will define a type of imprisonment that they will want to be freed from. The only escape, however, is to finish, and that's the point you need to make.

If their procrastination interferes with your plans, take them with you if you must, but when you return, back they go. *This must become a major inconvenience for them and not for you!* They will learn quickly that the work isn't going to go away and they could be doing something with their time that would be a lot more fun. If you have any problems getting them to help in the future, just remind them that it could be much worse and they'll know what you're talking about.

6 DOING THE JOB RIGHT: "It ain't over 'til it's over"

Once you've learned to get your children to get up and do a job, you might wonder why they don't do it properly. *You have to take the time to teach them.* What may seem easy and obvious to you will not necessarily be obvious to them.

You must set the standard by which each job will be judged. They will learn what that standard is only with your help. Try to have reasonable expectations based upon the age and ability of the child but at the same time don't allow the standard to be any lower than they're capable of achieving.

Once the standard has been established, let them know that you don't consider the job finished until they have done it properly. You don't want to teach them to just go through the motions. You want them to achieve a goal, and that goal will be to do the job right.

If you are convinced that all of this has been clearly communicated and you still have trouble getting them to do a job properly, try the following:

Step 1: Once they've begun to work, remind them of the result you expect. You want to maintain a pleasant tone, never giving them the impression that you expect them to do the job improperly. Just reminding them of all that's expected and leave them alone to do the work. Allow them the trust that expresses the attitude "I know you can do it."

Step 2: After they've finished to the best of their ability, go look at what they've accomplished. If the job was done well, praise them and you can both go about your business. But if the work isn't done well you'll need to do something about it.

This would be a good time to show them what else needs to be done or what needs to be done over. They might not be happy about it, but the job isn't done until it's done right. If the problem persists, for instance if the dishes are never clean when they finish and you're sure that they know how to do it properly, you can begin to be a little less understanding.

Explain to them that in the future, if the quality of the work doesn't improve, they'll be expected to redo the work and additional work besides. In the case of jobs that they take turns doing, they might be assigned everyone else's turn until they show you that they're willing to take the time to do it correctly. Then give them the chance.

Step 3: When they claim to be finished, check the work again. If they still haven't met the goals let them know that the consequence is now in effect.

For a period of time it will be necessary for you to check up on their work often, always praising them if its done well. Soon you'll be able to assume that they're doing everything properly and allow them to leave the job site without your approval.

It will always be easier for them to do a job halfway or improperly. To get them to willingly apply themselves, you'll need to convince them that it *does* matter, enough for you to follow through. As you check up, however, remember to praise the effort. Soon they'll begin to take pride in their accomplishments and set their own high standards. The only really positive incentive that they have is your acceptance and approval. Never miss an opportunity to give it to them even if it's only for the portion of the job that they did well but keep in mind that you're trying to teach the principle that 'it ain't over 'til it's over'.

 PICKING UP AFTER THEMSELVES: "Adam and Eve didn't have to put their clothes away."

As your children wander through your home, you may have noticed that they've developed a tendency to leave a trail of belongings strewn behind them as they go. If life seems to have become a never ending game of 'follow the leader' with them leading and dropping and you following and picking up and your scolding and complaining is falling upon deaf ears, maybe its time for you to try something more effective.

Its time to convince your offspring to pick up after themselves without a fuss! Realistically you'll seldom be able to avoid having to remind them to clean up their mess, but you can avoid the limited choices of arguing about it or doing it yourself. You will need to convince them that there will be a new third option that will exist today, tomorrow and forever. Soon you'll be able to put away your

"Adam and Eve didn't have to put their clothes away."

maid or butler's uniform no matter how good you look in it. You won't need it any longer.

Because there are so many objects that can be involved, I'll give examples of two of the most common problems. The system is the same for any situation but the consequences will need to change.

Example A (TOYS):
" Why can't they put it back?"

Step 1: Ask them politely to put the toy away.

Step 2: If it isn't done right away or if they refuse to do it, ask again adding that they won't be allowed to have another until it's done. Tell them also that if you have to do it they won't be able to play with any toy for a period of time specified by you.

Step 3: If after Step 2 nothing has been done, put the toy away and don't let them play with it just as you warned them. At first you might still feel like the maid, but remember that if you follow through with the consequence every time, things will improve.

Example B (Clothing):
"Adam and Eve

Step 1: Ask them nicely, as in example A.

Step 2: Again, if it isn't done or if you hear too much complaining, explain to them that if it isn't done soon and quietly, you'll pick up the clothes for them. Warn them that everything you find will be put into a 'special' box and they won't be able to wear that item for awhile. The period of time should be whatever you think it will take to get the message across.

Step 3: If after the second step they still complain or fail to do it, take the clothes in question and put them into the box. Label them with the next 'wear date' attached and don't let them wear them. Because they will most often be wearing the clothing they like, a favorite if you're lucky, the message will be an effective one. Don't give in later because they really need the clothes or because you feel sorry for them and you're not upset anymore. Mercy must never rob justice. This will work only if they learn that you have the emotional strength to follow through.

8 HOMEWORK: "My teacher must have made a mistake."

Let me guess. Your child's report card just arrived and it wasn't as good as you hoped it would be. Now they're cowering before you trying to explain that it wasn't their fault. Some teacher must have made a mistake! As they stand there waiting for the ax to fall, surprise them. Be understanding! Their college career isn't in jeopardy yet. You can still save the day!

There are many reasons for your student's grades to drop. Don't accuse them of stupidity or jump to the conclusion that there's been a decrease of effort on their part. A promotion to a higher grade (requiring more effort) can catch them by surprise. New opportunities for involvement in extracurricular activities, new friendships or a score of other valid reasons could be taking them away from their books. Before you can fully re-solve the problem, you'll need to assess what the reasons are.

Try to be aware that as they get older their lives get more complex. They'll probably need your help and understanding as they learn to deal with these changes. Don't automatically assume that they're 'just getting lazy'. If you can convey this attitude of respect and sympathy to their problem, it will make it much easier to help them make the adjustments necessary.

The most effective way to deal with this prob-lem requires that you have a discussion with the student at the beginning of each school year. This is the ideal time to apply Step One, asking kindly that they do whatever's necessary to maintain a level of success that you feel is appropriate with their ability. Later in the school year if problems occur, you can go to Step Two and Three knowing that they had their chance.

Step 1: As explained above, sit down with your child, in a concerned yet respectful manner, and set the goals that you both agree are reasonable. Let them know that you expect them to maintain those standards.

Step 2: If, at some time during the school year, you discover that the goals you both set are not being achieved, it becomes appropriate for you to sit down with them again to offer a solution. Because you've already given them a chance to organize their own lives, and they've been unsuccessful, you can now implement Step Two, the options.

Explain to them that you're disappointed that they were unable to do better but you understand. However, it will now be necessary for you to monitor their progress so they don't fall further behind.

The solution that you offer requires them to prepare a weekly schedule outlining the time they plan to set aside to do the homework and/or make up work that is necessary. They can do that work anytime they choose, but you will be checking to see that it's being done.

After you've reviewed their plan, explain that you expect them to stick to it. If they tell you that they don't have any homework or that they did it all in study hall (one of my favorites) they still have to spent the time reviewing. It must be made clear to them at this time that if they don't stay on this schedule, or if their grades don't improve, you plan to take over all control in deciding when they will study, until the standard has been met. Then, over the next few weeks, follow up in a positive way, reminding them and expressing pleasure and pride in the responsible way they're handling the problem.

NOTE: The amount of time needed to study should be based on their age and the amount of actual time that you feel will be required. This is not a punishment and should reflect only the actual effort necessary. Don't overreact in anger or frustration.

Step 3: If there seems to be no improvement, or if they aren't sticking to the schedule, take over for awhile. You decide when they study, even if it interferes with their social life or their favorite TV shows. Keep them on your study schedule until they bring home proof from school that their work is improving. Notes from teachers are best because

"If they're late often enough, they'll be due back before they leave

they can indicate areas where more work is needed.

If an improvement is noted, put them back on their schedule for awhile and see if it goes better this time. As they begin to succeed, they will feel a pride that will motivate them to stay with it. School will be more fun for them when they know the answers to the test questions and have their homework assignments completed.

It's important that you keep monitoring their progress from time to time. If they feel that you don't care enough to check up, it probably doesn't matter that much. In a nice way you want them to get the message that it matters very much. With the extra effort on both your parts they are going to find out that they're smarter than they thought they were but it won't be a surprise to you, after all they are your children.

9 CURFEW: "They could have danced all night."

No matter how much it frightens you to allow your children to spend time alone in the real world, there's no way to avoid it. One day they'll leave home with a date that, at least in your mind, is sure to corrupt them and destroy any future they might have had. These are natural thoughts for any parent and it won't do any good to tell you not to worry. Besides, you might be right. As they leave home your control becomes thin at best. You'll try to establish a reasonable time for them to return, but what happens when they don't come home when they're supposed to? As you sit in the dark fearing the worst and becoming more and more angry, try to calm down. You'll need to be under control if you expect to arrange any kind of understanding that will minimize your worry in the future.

The sooner you establish this understanding about curfew, the less you'll worry when worry becomes reasonable. Return times can be set and understood as soon as they're old enough to tell time. If a pattern is established early, they won't be as sensitive to it when they become capable of getting into real trouble. The deadline will be up to you both but the problem is, what do you do when they begin to consistently come in after curfew?

Note: My sons and I had an understanding but being a normal parent I was more concerned about the problems that my daughters could get into. Pamela, my oldest daughter, pointed out the unfairness of this policy and I had to agree with her. It didn't change anything, however.

When my children were going out I, like most parents, wanted to know when they planned to be home. Until they started to date we didn't have many problems, but the years that followed more than made up for it. No matter what we agreed to, their friends could always stay out later. It seemed that everyone they knew had more freedom than I was allowing them. In order to come to an agreement about what was reasonable, discussion was necessary. Weekdays were different than weekends. Prom nights were different than normal weekends and opening and closing nights of the school play needed yet a different agreement.

Be realistic and accept the fact that curfew will change for every different occasion. That's okay. You both need to be happy and discussing things like this might be the only time you get to see or talk to your children when they're this age. The problem to address is what to do when they don't get home when they agreed to. They will always have a good excuse but that won't save you from the worry inherent in parenting. The following example may help you limit your worry to a set time.

Step 1: Come to an agreement about the time that they should be home. Express your trust in them, (this will probably be an exaggeration but be as sincere as possible). Explain to them that your concern is about the many things that might happen to them that would be beyond their control. Be nice, polite and loving.

Step 2: If they don't want to come to an agreement or if they come in late, offer them this advice as a warning. Tell them that the next time they're late the existing curfew will be changed to one hour earlier and if they miss that curfew it will be put back another hour. If they're late enough times, they could be due back before they leave.

You can add hope as well by offering to consider a later curfew if they prove to be responsible adhering to the one that you've mutually set. All of this must seem fair and reasonable to them, so compromise a little if you have to.

Step 3: Wait up for them so that they know that you care and that you meant what you said. If they're late, inform them that in the future they will be expected to come home at the earlier time. Don't use anger in explaining this to them. They'll be angry and accuse you of being unfair, but that won't be true. You explained everything clearly and they understood. They're the ones that have been unfair.

Don't forget that if they do stick to the curfew and desire a little more freedom, you'll owe that to them as well. Fair is fair. Justice works both ways and if you keep your word you'll be establishing a trust that will help you resolve problems in the future. Maybe someday they'll be able to dance all night with a clear conscience and your blessing.

"Give them a little respect."

CHAPTER FIVE:
Some Parting Advice

Parenting can be fun or frustrating, it's up to you. In this book you've learned about a different way to deal with your children, a method requiring that you treat your children with respect. If you can accept that one of their greatest needs is your respect, you can have the happy home that you had always hoped for. If day to day pressures cause you to continue withholding that respect, you will have problems.

Our society bombards us with statements that lead us to believe that the fault is somehow inherent in childhood. Concepts like the 'generation gap' being normal seduce us into believing that the problems we have with our children are somehow unavoidable. If we accept these concepts, then the problems will be unavoidable. But there is another possibility.

We can choose to find a better way. We can choose to try to change ourselves if necessary. But we must believe that the relationship we hoped for is possible, and it is.

The Power of Respect is available to any parent who's willing to take the time and make the effort to change their parenting style. The desire for respect is a universal need and must be fulfilled if we want our children to develop to their full potential. If we don't give them respect as its deserved, our relationship with them will be limited or destroyed and it will inhibit their potential accomplishments.

If the withholding of respect in our youth controlled us, we can be controlled and limited as adults simply by the opinion of others. Some adults can need approval so badly that every decision becomes painful and success limited to what others say they are capable of achieving. But we don't need to pass that legacy on to our children. We can help them develop all the confidence they will ever need, simply by expressing our pride and faith in them as they grow up.

If you're not having fun as a parent, you're not doing it right. Coming home after work or seeing your children come home from school should be the most enjoyable part of your day. It *can* be like that.

I began work on this book the day my oldest son asked me why we got along so well. He told me that his friends didn't like going home and when they did, they fought with their parents. He wanted to know why our relationship was so special. I decided to write down the system and concept so that each of my children would have the knowledge they would need to be happy and successful parents when the time came.

The Power of Respect is the secret that no one has shared with us before. Now it belongs to everyone. Use it and be happy. I am and so are my children.

"The pencil can be mightier than the sword."

CHAPTER SIX:
The Journal

Now that you understand the system and are motivated to start solving problems, its time for you to begin stretching your imagination. The examples in the previous chapter were intended to demonstrate the practical application of The Power of Respect and give you a chance to test its effectiveness. This chapter is a workbook that challenges you to understand problems from your child's point of view and create consequences that vary with different situations, customized to both of your personalities.

As you apply the solutions you invent, keep in mind that all three steps of the system must be used when necessary, each time beginning with Step 1. Even if the problem reoccurs, do not start with Step 2 or 3 at any time or for any reason. If you exercise a little patience, your children will soon learn that it's best to respond to Step 1.

NOTE: If you create a successful or innovative consequence and would like to share it with others or if you're having a problem that you don't seem able to resolve and would like some suggestions please feel free to write the author at the following address:

The Power of Respect
Laser Print, Inc.
3483 South West Temple
Salt Lake City, Utah 84123

The problem: _____

_____

Possible reasons for the problem:

_____

_____

_____

_____

_____

_____

_____

Possible consequences:

_____

_____

_____

_____

_____

_____

_____

The problem: _____

_____

Possible reasons for the problem:

_____

_____

_____

_____

_____

_____

_____

Possible consequences:

_____

_____

_____

_____

_____

_____

_____

The problem: _____

_____

Possible reasons for the problem:

_____

_____

_____

_____

_____

_____

_____

Possible consequences:

_____

_____

_____

_____

_____

_____

_____

The problem: _____

_____

Possible reasons for the problem:

_____

_____

_____

_____

_____

_____

_____

Possible consequences:

_____

_____

_____

_____

_____

_____

_____

The problem: _____

_____

Possible reasons for the problem:

_____

_____

_____

_____

_____

_____

_____

Possible consequences:

_____

_____

_____

_____

_____

_____

_____

The problem: _____

_____

Possible reasons for the problem:

_____

_____

_____

_____

_____

_____

_____

Possible consequences:

_____

_____

_____

_____

_____

_____

_____

The problem: _____

_____

Possible reasons for the problem:

_____

_____

_____

_____

_____

_____

_____

Possible consequences:

_____

_____

_____

_____

_____

_____

_____

The problem: _____

_____

Possible reasons for the problem:

_____

_____

_____

_____

_____

_____

_____

Possible consequences:

_____

_____

_____

_____

_____

_____

_____

The problem: _____

_____

Possible reasons for the problem:

_____

_____

_____

_____

_____

_____

Possible consequences:

_____

_____

_____

_____

_____

_____

The problem: _____

_____

Possible reasons for the problem:

_____

_____

_____

_____

_____

_____

_____

Possible consequences:

_____

_____

_____

_____

_____

_____

_____

The problem: _____

_____

Possible reasons for the problem:

_____

_____

_____

_____

_____

_____

Possible consequences:

_____

_____

_____

_____

_____

_____

The problem: _____
_____

Possible reasons for the problem:
_____
_____
_____
_____
_____
_____
_____

Possible consequences:
_____
_____
_____
_____
_____
_____
_____

The problem: _____

_____

Possible reasons for the problem:

_____

_____

_____

_____

_____

_____

Possible consequences:

_____

_____

_____

_____

_____

_____

The problem: _____

_____

Possible reasons for the problem:

_____

_____

_____

_____

_____

_____

_____

Possible consequences:

_____

_____

_____

_____

_____

_____

_____

The problem: _____

_____

Possible reasons for the problem:

_____

_____

_____

_____

_____

_____

_____

Possible consequences:

_____

_____

_____

_____

_____

_____

_____

The problem: _____

_____

Possible reasons for the problem:

_____

_____

_____

_____

_____

_____

_____

Possible consequences:

_____

_____

_____

_____

_____

_____

_____

The problem: _____

_____

Possible reasons for the problem:

_____

_____

_____

_____

_____

_____

Possible consequences:

_____

_____

_____

_____

_____

_____

The problem: _____

_____

Possible reasons for the problem:

_____

_____

_____

_____

_____

_____

_____

Possible consequences:

_____

_____

_____

_____

_____

_____

_____

The problem: _____

_____

Possible reasons for the problem:

_____

_____

_____

_____

_____

_____

_____

Possible consequences:

_____

_____

_____

_____

_____

_____

_____

The problem: _____
_____

Possible reasons for the problem:

_____
_____
_____
_____
_____
_____
_____

Possible consequences:

_____
_____
_____
_____
_____
_____
_____

The problem: _____

_____

Possible reasons for the problem:

_____

_____

_____

_____

_____

_____

_____

Possible consequences:

_____

_____

_____

_____

_____

_____

_____

The problem: _____

_____

Possible reasons for the problem:

_____

_____

_____

_____

_____

_____

_____

Possible consequences:

_____

_____

_____

_____

_____

_____

_____

The problem: _____

_____

Possible reasons for the problem:

_____

_____

_____

_____

_____

_____

_____

Possible consequences:

_____

_____

_____

_____

_____

_____

_____

The problem: _____

_____

Possible reasons for the problem:

_____

_____

_____

_____

_____

_____

_____

Possible consequences:

_____

_____

_____

_____

_____

_____

_____

The problem: _____

_____

Possible reasons for the problem:

_____

_____

_____

_____

_____

_____

_____

Possible consequences:

_____

_____

_____

_____

_____

_____

_____

The problem: _____
_____

Possible reasons for the problem:

_____
_____
_____
_____
_____
_____
_____

Possible consequences:

_____
_____
_____
_____
_____
_____
_____

The problem: _____

_____

Possible reasons for the problem:

_____

_____

_____

_____

_____

_____

_____

Possible consequences:

_____

_____

_____

_____

_____

_____

_____

The problem: _____
_____

Possible reasons for the problem:
_____
_____
_____
_____
_____
_____
_____

Possible consequences:
_____
_____
_____
_____
_____
_____
_____

The problem: _____

_____

Possible reasons for the problem:

_____

_____

_____

_____

_____

_____

_____

Possible consequences:

_____

_____

_____

_____

_____

_____

_____

The problem: _____

_____

Possible reasons for the problem:

_____

_____

_____

_____

_____

_____

_____

Possible consequences:

_____

_____

_____

_____

_____

_____

_____

The problem: _____

_____

Possible reasons for the problem:

_____

_____

_____

_____

_____

_____

_____

Possible consequences:

_____

_____

_____

_____

_____

_____

_____

The problem: _____

_____

Possible reasons for the problem:

_____

_____

_____

_____

_____

_____

_____

Possible consequences:

_____

_____

_____

_____

_____

_____

_____

The problem: _____

_____

Possible reasons for the problem:

_____

_____

_____

_____

_____

_____

_____

Possible consequences:

_____

_____

_____

_____

_____

_____

_____

The problem: _____

_____

Possible reasons for the problem:

_____

_____

_____

_____

_____

_____

_____

Possible consequences:

_____

_____

_____

_____

_____

_____

_____

The problem: _____

_____

Possible reasons for the problem:

_____

_____

_____

_____

_____

_____

Possible consequences:

_____

_____

_____

_____

_____

_____

The problem: _____

_____

Possible reasons for the problem:

_____

_____

_____

_____

_____

_____

_____

Possible consequences:

_____

_____

_____

_____

_____

_____

_____

The problem: _____

_____

Possible reasons for the problem:

_____

_____

_____

_____

_____

_____

Possible consequences:

_____

_____

_____

_____

_____

_____

The problem: _____

_____

Possible reasons for the problem:

_____

_____

_____

_____

_____

_____

_____

Possible consequences:

_____

_____

_____

_____

_____

_____

_____

The problem: _____

_____

Possible reasons for the problem:

_____

_____

_____

_____

_____

_____

Possible consequences:

_____

_____

_____

_____

_____

_____

Photo by Gary (Rex) Bowers

ABOUT THE AUTHOR

P. Lawrence Wright, a national award winning artist and designer, is a single parent of five children and grandparent of four. His quest for more positive and effective parenting methods has lasted fourteen years culminating in his first published book "Parenting and the power of respect". He currently lives in Salt Lake City, Utah, with his two youngest children, Elizabeth and Katie. His oldest children, Michael, Sean and Pamela are married and have started families of their own.

Book Order Form

Individuals interested in purchasing a book directly from the publisher can use the order form below. Send check or money order (no cash or COD's please) to:

The Power of Respect
Laser Print, Inc.
3483 South West Temple
Salt Lake City, Utah, 84115

Number of books ordered_____ at $14.95 each plus $3.00 shipping and handling for each book ordered. I am inclosing $ _____ .

Name:_____
Address: _____
City:_____ State/zip_____
Signature:_____
Date: _____

Books are also available at quantity discounts for established groups or organizations promoting parenting counseling, classes or seminars. For more information please write to the publisher at the above address or call 1(801) 264-1166